# Henry Ossawa Tanner

*His Boyhood Dream Comes True*

Bunker Hill Publishing thanks the staff at the Pennsylvania Academy of the Fine Arts
for their contributions to this publication:

Anna Marley, Curator of Historical American Art;
Barbara Katus, Photo Archivist & Digital Assets Manager;
Judith Thomas, Manager of Rights & Reproductions.

www.bunkerhillpublishing.com

First published in 2011 by Bunker Hill Publishing Inc.
by Bunker Hill Publishing Inc.
285 River Road, Piermont
New Hampshire 03779, USA

10 8 6 4 2 3 5 7 9

Library of Congress Control Number: 2011925666

ISBN 13: 978-1-59373-092-5
ISBN 10: 1-59373-092-6

Published in the United States by Bunker Hill Publishing

Printed in China by Jade Productions

# Henry Ossawa Tanner
## *His Boyhood Dream Comes True*

Written and illustrated by Faith Ringgold

BUNKER HILL PUBLISHING

*in association with*

PENNSYLVANIA ACADEMY OF THE FINE ARTS

1. Henry Ossawa Tanner, 1907

2. Henry Ossawa Tanner at age 4

**3. The Tanner Family,** c. 1891
*Left to right:* Isabella, Halle, her daughter Sadie, Henry, Bishop Tanner,
Carlton, Mrs. Tanner, Bertha, Sarah and Mary

4. Henry Ossawa Tanner at age 20

Henry Ossawa Tanner was thirteen years old when he first realized he wanted to become an artist. Henry and his father were walking in Fairmount Park in Philadelphia close to their family home when they saw an artist painting. As they continued walking, Henry told his father about his dream.

*An artist? This boy can't be serious*, his father must have thought. It was 1872, and just eight years after the Civil War had ended. Most African Americans were still trying to overcome the legacy of more than two hundred years of slavery in America. Henry's father was not encouraging.

When Henry got home, he told his mother: "I want to be an artist. Just like the one I saw painting in the park."

The next day, Henry went back to Fairmount Park. Henry's mother had given him fifteen cents to buy dry pigments and used brushes to paint with. On that day, Henry probably got more paint on his clothes and on the ground than on his canvas, but he had started to live out his dream of becoming an artist.

Henry Ossawa Tanner was no ordinary young man. He was born in 1859, just two years before the Civil War began. His middle name, Ossawa, was taken from the town of Osawatomie in Kansas where John Brown, a leader in the anti-slavery movement, had led a raid against pro-slavery forces.

Henry's mother, Sarah Elizabeth Miller, was born a slave on May 18, 1840, in Virginia. She escaped from slavery on the Underground Railroad with the aid of the Pennsylvania Abolitionist Society. She came north and met Henry's father at Avery College in Allegheny City, Pennsylvania. The classmates married in 1858. Sarah was a gentle, loving mother. You can see Henry's love for his mother in a portrait he painted of her in 1897.

5. *Portrait of the Artist's Mother,* 1897

Henry's father, Benjamin
Tucker Tanner, was born free
in Pittsburgh on Christmas Day
in 1835. He became a minister
and later a bishop in the African
Methodist Episcopal Church.

6. *Benjamin Tucker Tanner,* 1897

Henry was the oldest of seven children. The Tanner family was a model of strength, love, and accomplishment at a time when most Black people in America had very little or nothing to look forward to, not even their own personal freedom.

The Tanner Family, c. 1891

In 1877, Henry graduated from the Roberts Vaux Grammar School, one of the only secondary schools for Black students in Philadelphia. Henry was elected to deliver the valedictory address. His topic was "Compulsory Education."

Henry continued his studies at the Pennsylvania Academy of the Fine Arts, the most reputable art college in America. His teacher was Thomas Eakins, a celebrated American portrait painter. Eakins taught Henry drawing and painting from the model, and life study.

Henry often went to the Philadelphia Zoo to draw and paint the animals there. The lions were among his favorite subjects. They appear in many of his paintings along with other animals. Henry had thought at one time that he would be the world's greatest animal painter.

7. *Pomp at the Zoo,* c. 1880

8. *Sand Dunes at Sunset, Atlantic City,* c. 1885

But Henry also loved to paint the ocean, the beach, and ships at sea. Maybe he would be the world's greatest marine painter, and win a coveted acceptance to the Paris Salon. Little did Henry know that in 1996, more than a hundred years after he painted *Sand Dunes at Sunset, Atlantic City,* it would hang in the East Wing of the White House, at the request of President and Mrs. Clinton. It would be the first painting by an African American artist to take its place beside works by some of the greatest American painters of that time, including Gilbert Stuart, Winslow Homer, Mary Cassatt, John Singer Sargent, James McNeill Whistler, and Henry's teacher at the Pennsylvania Academy of the Fine Arts, Thomas Eakins.

15

Henry longed to go to Europe, where he had heard that a Black artist could be accepted without prejudice. He needed funds to travel and study there, however. So he took a job teaching at Clark College in Atlanta, where he met Bishop Joseph Crane Hartzell and his wife, friends of Henry's father. The Hartzells arranged an exhibition for Henry in Cincinnati, but when no paintings were sold, the Hartzells bought all of them. Henry now had his first show and his first patrons. His dream was taking form.

**9.** *Bishop Joseph Crane Hartzell,* 1902

**10. American Art Club,** c. 1900
Tanner seated in first row, fourth from left

Henry sailed from New York to Paris, where he joined the American Art Students' Club of Paris and took classes at the Académie Julian. He spent his first summer in Paris painting landscapes. It was 1891, and Henry was at last in the center of the art world.

All around him was the glorious life of creativity and the freedom to paint. And in Paris, the color of Henry's skin would not stand in the way of his dream of becoming a famous artist.

11. *The Seine,* c. 1902

Unfortunately, Henry developed typhoid fever. He had to return to the United States to rest and recuperate.

Once he recovered from his illness, Henry resumed painting. His subject was African American life. His first painting was *The Banjo Lesson*, which depicted an old man teaching a young boy to play the banjo, a popular musical instrument in the South at the time. As was his custom, Henry made several studies from models to help him capture the scene.

Another painting Henry did at this time was *The Thankful Poor,* for which he also used models. These were his only paintings based on African American themes. When he returned to Paris in 1895, *The Banjo Lesson* was accepted at the salon. It was the first time any of his works had been exhibited there. From then on, for the next twenty years, Henry Tanner's work would be accepted each year at the Paris Salon. His return to Paris was triumphant.

12. *The Banjo Lesson,* 1893

In Paris, Henry began painting Bible stories that he had read as a child. In *Daniel in the Lions' Den*, Henry got to paint one of his favorite animals, the lion. It was for this painting that Henry received an honorable mention at the Paris Salon for the first time. He was inspired to work even harder to achieve his ultimate dream to become a celebrated artist.

**14.** *Daniel in the Lions' Den*, 1907-1918

*The Resurrection of Lazarus,* Henry's most famous religious painting, was another in a series of many religious paintings that were also accepted at the salon. These works established Henry as a painter of religious themes.

15. *The Resurrection of Lazarus,* 1896

In 1898, Henry met Jessie McCauley Olssen in Paris. Jessie was an American music student of Swedish ancestry who'd come to Europe to study voice. Henry and Jessie became friends, fell in love, and—on December 14, 1899—were married.

16. **Henry Ossawa Tanner,** 1907, and **Jessie Olssen Tanner,** c. 1890

24

Henry and Jessie returned to America. On September 25, 1903, in New York City, they had a son whom they named Jesse, after his mother. Henry's son, Jesse, and his wife, Jessie, would serve as models in many of his paintings.

**17. Jessie Olssen Tanner** and **Jesse Ossawa Tanner,** c. 1908

Through his artistic career, Henry painted in many genres. His father, Bishop Tanner, would have been pleased to know that in Europe and America, Henry's religious paintings were the most celebrated of all his works.

**18.** *Edge of the Forest,* c. 1893

By now it was clear to everyone that Henry's struggle to become an artist in one of the most difficult periods in American history was realized. For years to come, his life was a model for other African American artists.

In 1909, he was elected an associate member of the National Academy of Design in America. When he was elected a full member in 1927, he presented *The Miraculous Haul of Fishes* as his reception piece.

**19.** *The Miraculous Haul of Fishes,*
c. 1913-1914

In America, the Harlem Renaissance was in full bloom, but African American artists still traveled to Europe, where they enjoyed a freedom that did not exist at home. They also came to meet the famous African American painter Henry Ossawa Tanner.

20. **Chevalier of the Legion of Honor,** 1923

On August 17, 1923, Henry received the chevalier of the Legion of Honor, France's highest award for an artist. By now, Henry had become the first African American painter to be celebrated in both America and Europe. His boyhood dream had finally come true.

21. Henry Ossawa Tanner with palette, c. 1935

# Picture credits

**1 and 16a:** Henry Ossawa Tanner, 1907
Frederick Gutekunst, photographer.
Henry Ossawa Tanner Papers, Archives of
American Art, Smithsonian Institution,
Washington, DC.

**2:** Henry Ossawa
Tanner at age 4
Smithsonian American
Art Museum,
Photo Archives,
Washington DC.

**3:** The Tanner
Family, c 1891
Courtesy of Dr.
Rae Alexander-
Minter.

**4:** Henry Ossawa Tanner at age 20
Smithsonian American Art Museum,
Photo Archives, Washington, DC.

**5:** *Portrait of the Artist's Mother*, 1897
Philadelphia Museum of Art, Philadelphia, PA,
Partial gift of Dr. Rae Alexander-Minter and purchased with
the W. P. Wilstach Fund, the George W. Elkins Fund, the
Edward and Althea Budd Fund, and with funds contributed
by The Dietrich Foundation, 1993, EW 1993-61-1

**6:** *Benjamin Tucker Tanner*, 1897
Private Collection of Eddie C. and C. Sylvia Brown
Photo credit: Joseph Hyde

**7:** *Pomp at the Zoo*, c. 1880
Collection of Lewis Tanner Moore
Photo credit: Rick Echelmeyer

**8:** *Sand Dunes at Sunset, Atlantic City*, c. 1885
White House Historical Association
(White House Collection): 210, Washington, DC.

**9:** *Bishop Joseph Crane Hartzell*, 1902
Collection of Hampton University Museum,
Hampton, VA.

**10:** American Art Club, c. 1900
Unidentified photographer.
Henry Ossawa Tanner Papers, Archives
of American Art, Smithsonian Institution,
Washington, DC.

**11:** *The Seine*, c. 1902
National Gallery of Art, Washington DC.
Gift of the Avalon Foundation, 1971.57.1

**12:** *The Banjo Lesson,* 1893
Collection of Hampton University Museum,
Hampton, VA.

**13:** *The Thankful Poor,* 1894
Collection of Camille O. and William H. Cosby, Jr.
Photo credit: Frank Stewart

**14:** *Daniel in the Lions' Den,* 1907-1918
Los Angeles County Museum of Art, Los Angeles, CA.
Mr. and Mrs. William Preston Harrison Collection
(22.6.3). Digital Image ©2009 Museum Associates /
LACMA / Art Resource, NY.

**15:** *The Resurrection of Lazarus,* 1896
Musée d'Orsay, Paris, France, Inv. RF1980-173.
Photo: Hervé Lewandoswki. Photo credit: Réunion des Musées
Nationaux / Art Resource, NY.

**16b:** Jessie Olssen Tanner, c. 1890
Unidentified photographer.
Henry Ossawa Tanner Papers, Archives
of American Art, Smithsonian Institution,
Washington, DC.

**17:** Jessie Olssen Tanner and
Jesse Ossawa Tanner, c. 1908
Unidentified photographer.
Henry Ossawa Tanner Papers, Archives
of American Art, Smithsonian Institution,
Washington, DC.

**18:** *Edge of the Forest,* c. 1893
Collection of Michael Rosenfeld and
halley k harrisburg, New York, NY.

**19:** *The Miraculous Haul of Fishes,* c. 1913-1914
National Academy Museum,
New York, NY, 1236-P

**20:** Chevalier of the Legion of Honor, 1923

**21:** Henry Ossawa Tanner with palette, c. 1935
L. Matthes, photographer.
Henry Ossawa Tanner Papers, Archives
of American Art, Smithsonian Institution,
Washington, DC.

This book is published in conjunction with the exhibition *Henry Ossawa Tanner: Modern Spirit*, organized by the Pennsylvania Academy of the Fine Arts in Philadelphia, and presented January 27–April 15, 2012. The exhibit is also appearing at the Cincinnati Art Museum (May 26–September 9, 2012), and the Museum of Fine Arts, Houston (October 14, 2012–January 6, 2013).

We thank Lewis Tanner Moore and Dr. Rae Alexander-Minter, two Tanner family members, for their careful readings of this text and thoughtful editorial suggestions.

Exhibition Presenting Foundation sponsors:
**The Terra Foundation for American Art**, and the **Henry Luce Foundation**.

This exhibition has been made possible in part by the **National Endowment for the Humanities:** *Because democracy demands wisdom*.

Leading support from the **Mr. & Mrs. Raymond J. Horowitz Foundation for the Arts, Inc.**

*Philadelphia venue funding:*
Presenting Philadelphia Area Sponsor: **Exelon Foundation**.
Major corporate support from **PECO**.
Participating support from the **Edna W. Andrade Fund of the Philadelphia Foundation**.

Any views, findings, conclusions, or recommendations expressed in this exhibition and publication do not necessarily represent those of the National Endowment for the Humanities.